MIGHTY CONSTRUCTION MACHINES

DUMP TRUCKS

RYAN JAMES

A Crabtree Roots Book

Crabtree Publishing
crabtreebooks.com

School-to-Home Support for Caregivers and Teachers

This book helps children grow by letting them practice reading. Here are a few guiding questions to help the reader with building his or her comprehension skills. Possible answers appear here in red.

Before Reading:

- What do I think this book is about?
  - *I think this book is about how dump trucks work.*
  - *I think this book is about how dump trucks are made.*
- What do I want to learn about this topic?
  - *I want to learn what dump trucks do.*
  - *I want to learn the parts of a dump truck.*

During Reading:

- I wonder why...
  - *I wonder why some jobs need a dump truck.*
  - *I wonder why dump trucks have such big wheels.*
- What have I learned so far?
  - *I have learned that some dump trucks have four wheels.*
  - *I have learned that some dump trucks are yellow.*

After Reading:

- What details did I learn about this topic?
  - *I have learned that some dump trucks move dirt.*
  - *I have learned that all dump trucks have an open bed.*
- Read the book again and look for the vocabulary words.
  - *I see the word **wheels** on page 6 and the word **dirt** on page 8. The other vocabulary words are found on page 14.*

This is a **dump truck.**

Some dump trucks are yellow.

Some dump trucks have four **wheels**.

2887

Some dump trucks move **dirt**.

All dump trucks have an **open bed**.

How many dump trucks do you see?

Word List

Sight Words

a	four	see
all	have	some
an	how	this
are	is	yellow
do	many	you

Words to Know

dirt

dump truck

open bed

wheels

35 Words

This is a **dump truck**.

Some dump trucks are yellow.

Some dump trucks have four **wheels**.

Some dump trucks move **dirt**.

All dump trucks have an **open bed**.

How many dump trucks do you see?

MIGHTY CONSTRUCTION MACHINES

DUMP TRUCKS

RYAN JAMES

Written by: Ryan James
Designed by: Rhea Wallace
Series Development: James Earley
Proofreader: Melissa Boyce
Educational Consultant: Marie Lemke M.Ed.

Photographs:
Shutterstock: dragunov: cover; Sanit Fuanghakhen: p. 1; Dmytro Budnik: p.3; ABUtyrin22: p. 5;nurkhann: p. 9; Avigator Fortuner: p. 10-11; Nordroden: p. 13

Crabtree Publishing

crabtreebooks.com 800-387-7650

Printed in Canada/012024/CP20231127

Published in Canada
Crabtree Publishing
616 Welland Ave.
St. Catharines, Ontario
L2M 5V6

Published in the United States
Crabtree Publishing
347 Fifth Ave
Suite 1402-145
New York, NY 10016

Library and Archives Canada Cataloguing in Publication
Available at Library and Archives Canada

Library of Congress Cataloging-in-Publication Data
Available at the Library of Congress

Hardcover: 978-1-0398-3836-9
Paperback: 978-1-0398-3921-2
Ebook (pdf): 978-1-0398-4004-1
Epub: 978-1-0398-4076-8